WITHDRAWN

WOMEN SPORTS STARS

Carli Lloyd
Soccer Star

by Heather E. Schwartz

CAPSTONE PRESS
a capstone imprint

Snap Books are published by Capstone Press,
1710 Roe Crest Drive, North Mankato, Minnesota 56003
www.mycapstone.com

Copyright ©2018 by Capstone Press, a Capstone imprint. All rights reserved.
No part of this publication may be reproduced in whole or in part, or stored
in a retrieval system, or transmitted in any form or by any means, electronic,
mechanical, photocopying, recording, or otherwise, without written
permission of the publisher.

**Cataloging-in-Publication Data is on file at the Library of Congress
website.**
ISBN: 978-1-5157-9710-4 (library binding)
ISBN: 978-1-5157-9714-2 (paperback)
ISBN: 978-1-5157-9718-0 (eBook PDF)

Editorial Credits

Abby Colich, editor; Kayla Rossow, designer; Eric Gohl, media researcher;
Katy LaVigne, production specialist

Photo Credits

AP Photo: 24, Mel Evans, 11; Dreamstime: Scott Anderson, 23; Getty Images:
Stringer/Jamie Sabau, 7, Stringer/Ombrello/Nils Petter Nilsson, cover;
Newscom: Cal Sport Media/Mohammad Khursheed, 17, CNImaging/Gary,
15, Icon SMI/Scott Bales, 13, Reuters/Mariana Bazo, 26, SIPA/XINHUA, 5, 21,
ZUMA Press/Carl Sandin, 19, ZUMA Press/Paul Childs, 29; Shutterstock:
Erin Cadigan, 9 (all), irin-k, cover (background), Lev Radin, 3

Design Elements: Shutterstock

Printed and bound in the USA.
010780S18

Table of Contents

CHAPTER 1

Historic Hat Trick

The final match in the 2015 Women's World Cup was underway. The United States played against Japan. The game had barely started. Midfielder Carli Lloyd scored her first goal. The crowd went wild, but Carli was far from finished.

Minutes later she scored another goal. Then she saw a chance to do it again. The ball was loose in the middle of the field. She was positioned perfectly to launch it toward the goal. Carli scored from 54 yards (49 meters) away. It was her third goal in 16 minutes.

Carli jogged across the field, raising her arms and smiling widely. The fans screamed. Carli jumped and hugged her teammates. She was the first woman to score a hat trick in a World Cup final.

FACT

A hat trick is when a player scores three goals in a row in one game.

Carli (far right) celebrates a goal with her teammates at the 2015 World Cup finals.

CHAPTER 2

Competitive Kid

Carli Anne Lloyd was born July 16, 1982, in Delran, New Jersey. She began playing soccer at age 5. She loved it so much that she carried a soccer ball with her everywhere. She practiced her kicks on a local field.

Soccer wasn't the only sport Carli enjoyed. She spent hours playing basketball, baseball, and hockey with the neighborhood kids. She brought a competitive spirit to every sport she played. She always wanted to be the best.

Growing up, Carli sometimes felt like being sporty made her different from other girls. By high school, however, she was excited to be an athlete. She played for the Medford Strikers Soccer Club as well as her high school team. *The Philadelphia Inquirer* named her the girls' High School Player of the Year twice.

MAGNIFICENT MIDFIELDER

Carli's position on the field is center midfielder. It is a role that requires attacking to score goals. It also requires defensive play to keep the other team from scoring. She is responsible for organizing plays among her teammates.

As a kid, it's really hard to go through those times of being a teenager, and I know when I was really active it was looked upon as, 'Well, you're not girly enough.' So it was hard going through that, but once I reached the high school level, it was really cool to be an athlete. I think that's when I started to really embrace it and own it and enjoy it.

—Carli Lloyd to *USA Today*, July 6, 2015

Carli with her parents and brother in 2011

CHAPTER 3

Successes and Struggles

In 2001 Carli began college at Rutgers University in New Jersey. She was a standout on the soccer team. As a freshman, she was the 2001 Big East Rookie of the Year. It was the first time the honor ever went to a Rutgers player.

Throughout her time at Rutgers, Carli racked up many awards. She was an All-American three times. She was the first player in school history to earn First-Team All-Big East Honors four years in a row.

FACT

Carli earned a bachelor's degree in Exercise Science and Sport Studies from Rutgers.

From 2001 to 2003, Carli also played for the
U.S. Under-21 National Team. She was aiming for a
spot on the senior Women's National Team. Members
of this team have the chance to play in the FIFA
Women's World Cup and the Olympics.

In 2003 Carli was dealt a devastating blow. She
was cut from the Under-21 National Team. The coach
told her she still had some improvements to make.

Getting More Serious

Success in soccer had always come easily to Carli. When it didn't, she wanted to quit. She decided to play out her last year of college. Then she would pursue a career outside of sports. She thought about becoming an FBI agent. Only support from her family and a new coach could change her mind.

Carli's dad stepped in. He got in touch with James Galanis, a player and coach from Australia. Galanis ran a soccer academy in New Jersey.

Galanis believed in Carli. He said he would train her for free but that he wouldn't go easy on her. The first thing he did was call her out. He told her she wasn't playing her best. She was physically and mentally weak, but he had plans to change that.

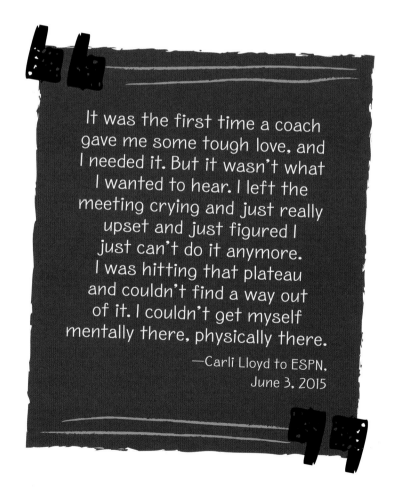

It was the first time a coach gave me some tough love, and I needed it. But it wasn't what I wanted to hear. I left the meeting crying and just really upset and just figured I just can't do it anymore. I was hitting that plateau and couldn't find a way out of it. I couldn't get myself mentally there, physically there.

—Carli Lloyd to ESPN, June 3, 2015

Carli was willing to do whatever it took. She worked harder than she ever had. She stopped making excuses. Galanis trained her to shoot for the goal from 50 yards (45.7 m) away. Carli thought it was a silly exercise. No one would shoot from so far away in a game. But she kept at it, trying and missing again and again.

Carli with James Galanis in 2012

From College to Pro

Carli finished her college career in 2004. She was a semifinalist for the Hermann Trophy her senior year. This honor goes to the top student-athlete soccer player. She was also the 2004 Big East Midfielder of the Year. Carli graduated from Rutgers as the all-time leader in points and goals.

Now it was time to focus on playing as a pro. With Galanis on her side, Carli made the U.S. senior National Team in 2005. She was now a pro player.

Carli found success as a pro. She was a starter for her team at the Algarve Cup, an annual tournament in Portugal, in 2006. The next year Carli scored four goals at the same tournament. Her play there earned her the honor of Most Valuable Player.

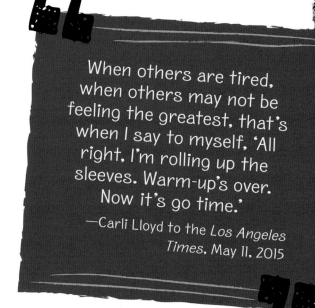

When others are tired, when others may not be feeling the greatest, that's when I say to myself, 'All right, I'm rolling up the sleeves. Warm-up's over. Now it's go time.'
—Carli Lloyd to the *Los Angeles Times*, May 11, 2015

In 2007 Carli made her FIFA Women's World Cup debut. Her team finished in third place. The year also marked a personal victory for Carli. She was the third-best scorer on her team, with nine goals to her credit. Her hard work at the sport she loved was paying off.

FACT

Becoming a starter is a big step. It means the player gets to play at the start of the game. Usually the best players in each position are starters.

Carli shoots the ball in a 2005 National Team game.

CHAPTER 4

Life as a Pro

In 2008 head coach Pia Sundhage named Carli to the U.S. Olympic Team. Carli would play in the Games in Beijing, China!

Carli had some amazing moments at the 2008 Olympics. In a match against Japan, she scored the game's only goal, securing a win for her team. Team USA played Brazil on a rainy, slippery field in the final match of the Games. Neither team scored for 90 minutes. The game went into overtime. Six minutes in, Carli took a shot with her left foot. She aimed for the lower left corner of the goal. Score! Carli's game-winning goal helped earn the team a gold medal. Carli later was named U.S. Soccer Female Athlete of the Year in 2008.

FACT

Only the best are named U.S. Soccer Female Athlete of the Year. It's the highest honor awarded to U.S. female soccer players.

The 2008 U.S. Olympic Team celebrates a gold medal win.

Carli was on a roll with her pro career. However, during the 2011 World Cup finals, she missed a penalty shot. The team lost to Japan. As she prepared for another Olympics in 2012, her coach lost faith in her. Then, the worst happened. Carli was benched. She would not be starting in the opening game.

Carli was shocked. This time, though, she wasn't about to give up.

Quick Comeback

Carli wasn't benched for long. In the first 16 minutes of the 2012 Olympic opening game, a teammate became injured. The coach put in Carli. She now had the chance to prove herself. She didn't disappoint. Carli scored the winning goal in a game against France.

Now that she was back in the starting lineup, Carli was ready to attack. She kept up her game right to the end. The pressure was on in the final game against Japan. The team had its 2008 Olympic gold to defend. Carli and her teammates hadn't forgotten the World Cup loss to Japan the previous year. More than 80,000 fans were watching Team USA.

Carli was on her game. She scored her team's only two goals. Team USA won another Olympic gold!

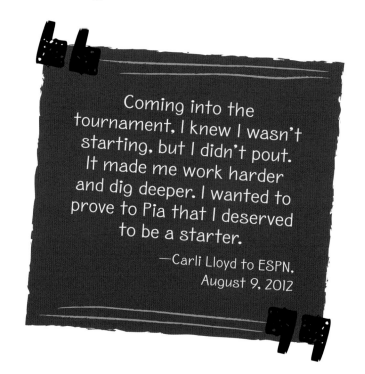

Coming into the tournament, I knew I wasn't starting, but I didn't pout. It made me work harder and dig deeper. I wanted to prove to Pia that I deserved to be a starter.

—Carli Lloyd to ESPN, August 9, 2012

Carli in a 2012 Olympic game against France

HEROIC HOMECOMING

Carli's community back in Delran, New Jersey, was very proud of its Olympic star. When Carli returned home, the town had a parade for her. They gave her a key to the city. She was honored in other ways too. She threw out the first pitch at a Phillies baseball game. Carli's success on the field had made her a local hero and celebrity.

Record Scoring

Carli was clearly showing her talent, but that didn't mean the wins were always easy. She still had to work hard for every goal and every win.

I'm a winner, and I want to go out there and win.

—Carli Lloyd to Sports Illustrated, March 4, 2015

In a 2013 National Team game against New Zealand, Carli power kicked the ball. It sailed past the goalie and right into the goal. It was Carli's 46th international goal. The United States won the game. The goal made Carli the top-scoring midfielder in the history of the U.S. National Team.

In 2014 the National Team came in a crushing seventh place in the Algarve Cup. Carli and her teammates were disappointed. The next year the team did not get off to a great start. They immediately lost two important games. Carli decided she'd had enough defeat. In a game against Norway, she raced toward the center of the field. She blasted the ball into the goal with her left foot. A few minutes later, Carli took a penalty shot. She nailed it — straight and high into the goal. The United States beat Norway 2–1. They went on to win the tournament.

The 2015 Algarve Cup champions

More World Cup Wins

A few months after the 2015 Algarve Cup, Carli and her team played in the World Cup. It was here that Carli would score the incredible history-making hat trick. She also became the first player in Women's National Team history to score in four straight World Cup games. She earned the Golden Ball, an award for the most valuable player in the tournament.

Carli wasn't in it just for herself. Her goals earned the U.S. team the World Cup title. The United States became the first country ever to have won three FIFA Women's World Cup titles. It was an honor shared by Carli, her teammates, and their country. President Barack Obama tweeted his congratulations to Carli. The team later visited the White House.

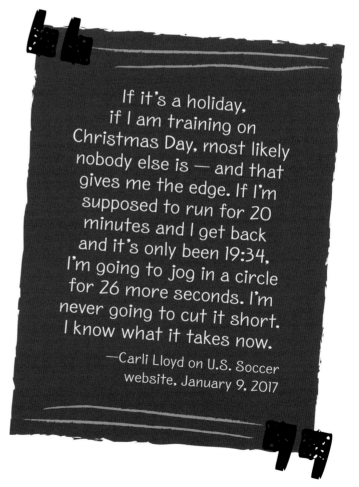

If it's a holiday, if I am training on Christmas Day, most likely nobody else is — and that gives me the edge. If I'm supposed to run for 20 minutes and I get back and it's only been 19:34, I'm going to jog in a circle for 26 more seconds. I'm never going to cut it short. I know what it takes now.

—Carli Lloyd on U.S. Soccer website, January 9, 2017

Carli with her Golden Ball trophy after the 2015 World Cup

FACT

In international competitions, soccer is called football. Only Americans use the word "soccer" to avoid confusion with American football.

MAKING HISTORY AT HOME

The U.S. Women's National Team was honored with a ticker-tape parade in New York City after its World Cup win. It was the first ticker-tape parade ever held in the city for a women's sports team. Carli told reporters she felt like they were making history.

CHAPTER 5

Creating a Legacy

After the 2015 World Cup win, Carli was recognized as a role model for other young female athletes. She felt it was important to inspire future generations. She wanted to set a good example.

One way she gave back was by hosting the 2015 Carli Lloyd Soccer Camp, in Medford, New Jersey. It was open to students ages 9 to 18. About 200 girls came to practice their skills. It was the same field where Carli played for the Medford Strikers Soccer Club. Her trainer, James Galanis, ran the camp. Carli was there to teach the girls the same drills she did as a young player. The young athletes also learned about using mental skills in soccer.

FACT

When Carli's not busy with the U.S. National Team, she plays in the National Women's Soccer League (NWSL). The league began in 2012 and consists of 10 teams. Carli began playing for the Houston Dash in 2015. Previously she played for the New York Flash.

> "I want to build my own unique legacy, one that's a role model on and off the field, somebody that a parent would want their kid looking up to. I think that people are slowly starting to see what I can do on the field and really respect my game, and that's what I want. I don't want to be known for someone that's good-looking. I want to be known as someone who is one of the best midfielders. That's my thing."
>
> —Carli Lloyd to ESPN, June 3, 2015

Off the field, Carli talks to young girls about her life.

Fighting for Fair Pay

In 2016 Carli took up a new cause that affected female athletes. Along with four teammates, she filed a wage-discrimination complaint against U.S. Soccer. Carli, Hope Solo, Becky Sauerbrunn, Alex Morgan, and Megan Rapinoe said U.S. Soccer unfairly paid female soccer players less than male soccer players. Female athletes had a guaranteed salary, but male athletes were paid more for wins.

(top row from left to right) Carli Lloyd, Alex Morgan, and Megan Rapinoe; (bottom row) Becky Sauerbrunn (left) and Hope Solo

U.S. Soccer fought back, but Carli and her teammates stuck to their guns. They spoke out in the media. Carli wrote an essay for *The New York Times*. In it she explained that the lawsuit wasn't just about herself and her team. It was for future female athletes. She was more than a role model on the field. She felt it was her job to fight for equal pay as a pro athlete too.

In April 2017 U.S. Soccer agreed to increase pay for female soccer players over five years. They still would not be paid as much as male soccer players. But Carli was happy they'd reached an agreement. It was a step in the right direction.

FACT

In 2015 the U.S. Women's National Team made more money than the men's team for the U.S. Soccer Federation. About $20 million more! Yet the female athletes were still only paid about 25 percent of what male players were paid.

Olympic Loss

By the time Carli went to the 2016 Olympics, she said her hat trick at the World Cup was "old news." She didn't want to look back on her previous success. She was ready to prove herself all over again. Carli wanted to play well and win another gold medal for the United States.

Carli scored in the first two games of the tournament. Despite her efforts, the U.S. team didn't win any medals. She vowed to do better at the 2019 World Cup and the 2020 Olympic Games. Her legacy was on the line. She planned to retire in just a few years.

SPORTY SWEETHEARTS

Although training, traveling, and playing soccer take up a lot of Carli's time, she manages to have a personal life too. She married her high school sweetheart, Brian Hollins, in November 2016. They have a love of sports in common. Brian is a professional golf player.

Carli with members of the 2016 U.S. Olympic Team

FACT

Most female players retire from the U.S. Women's National Team in their 30s. Christie Pearce retired at age 41 in 2017.

New Team, Same Goals

By 2017 Carli was well on her way to creating the legacy she wanted to leave as a soccer player. She started the year by accepting the 2016 award for Best FIFA Women's Player. She also signed on to play for Manchester City, a soccer team in England. She was eager to improve her game. Playing with new teammates and a new coach would help. She returned to the United States in June to begin the season with the Houston Dash.

When asked what she might like to do after retiring from soccer, Carli said she was interested in commentating. But for now she is still in the game. She has her eye on more immediate goals. She wants to win the next World Cup and Olympics.

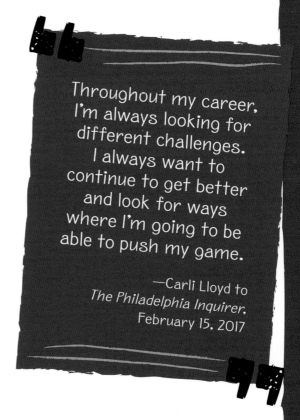

Throughout my career, I'm always looking for different challenges. I always want to continue to get better and look for ways where I'm going to be able to push my game.

—Carli Lloyd to
The Philadelphia Inquirer,
February 15, 2017

Carli in action with
Manchester City in 2017

FACT

Pro players have plenty of time to prepare for the biggest
international competitions. The World Cup and Olympic Games
are each held every four years.

Timeline

1982 ·· born in Delran, New Jersey, on July 16

2001 ·· begins playing for Rutgers

·· named Big East Rookie of the Year

2001 ·· begins playing for the U.S. Under-21 National Team

2003 ·· is cut from the Under-21 National Team

·· begins training with James Galanis

2004 ·· named semifinalist for the Hermann Trophy

·· named Big East Midfielder of the Year

·· graduates from Rutgers University

2005 ·· makes the U.S. Women's National Team

2006 ·· starts for her team at the Algarve Cup

2007 ·· scores four goals at Algarve Cup; earns MVP

·· makes her FIFA Women's World Cup debut

2008 ·· makes the Olympic Team and scores to win her team the gold medal

·· named U.S. Soccer Female Athlete of the Year

2011 ·· plays in World Cup finals

2012 ·· scores to win her team another gold medal at the 2012 Olympics

2013 ·· becomes the top-scoring midfielder in the history of the U.S. National Team

2015 ·· makes history with a hat trick at the World Cup

2017 ·· begins playing for Manchester City

Read More

Fishman, Jon M. *Carli Lloyd*. Amazing Athletes. Minneapolis: Lerner, 2016.

Lloyd, Carli. *All Heart: My Dedication and Determination to Become One of Soccer's Best.* Boston: Houghton Mifflin Harcourt, 2016.

Raum, Elizabeth. *Carli Lloyd*. Pro Sports Biographies. Mankato, Minn.: Amicus, 2018.

Internet Sites

Use FactHound to find Internet sites related to this book.

Visit *www.facthound.com*

Just type in 9781515797104 and go!

 Super-cool stuff! Check out projects, games and lots more at **www.capstonekids.com**

Index